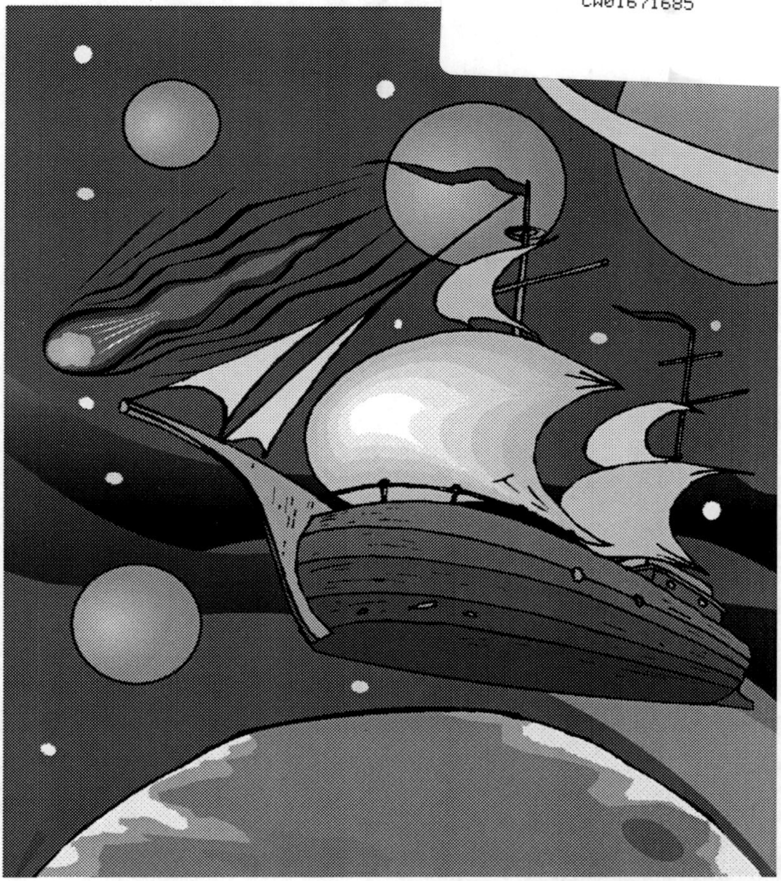

2001: A POETRY ODYSSEY EAST & WEST CORNWALL

Edited by Heather Killingray

First published in Great Britain in 2001 by
YOUNG WRITERS
Remus House,
Coltsfoot Drive,
Peterborough, PE2 9JX
Telephone (01733) 890066

HB ISBN 0 75432 942 9
SB ISBN 0 75432 943 7

FOREWORD

Young Writers was established in 1991 with the aim to promote creative writing in children, to make reading and writing poetry fun.

This year the 2001: A Poetry Odyssey competition again proved to be a tremendous success with over 50,000 entries received nationwide.

The amount of hard work and effort put into each entry impressed us all, and is reflective of the teaching skills in schools today.

The task of selecting poems for publication was a difficult one but nevertheless, an enjoyable experience. We hope you are as pleased with the final selection in *2001: A Poetry Odyssey East & West Cornwall* as we are.

CONTENTS

The Poems

WATCHER

I saw him standing,
Where he always does.
As he always has.
Like he always will.
A rock in the ground,
Child of the earth,
Yet not belonging.
Not here,
Only in body.
The mind is in
Another place,
Another time.
But blending in,
Not a figure, alone
On the landscape -
Just a shade in the
Simple picture,
Invisibly interacting,
Human chameleon.
Looking out,
Towards the future,
Facing the past,
Ignoring the present.
Seeing all, though
Believing nothing.
I saw him standing,
Where he always does,
As he always has,
Like he always will.

Jemma King (15)
Cape Cornwall School

The Olympics

As the Olympic torch was being lit,
all the athletes were still training, getting fit.

Denise Lewis won the heptathalon
and she is still going strong.

We came and got gold in the veladrome
and happily went home.

We got gold in the rowing
and we were still going.

We got silver in the javelin
and we are not going to give in.

The closing ceremony with fireworks
was breathtaking as we had watched
our athletes record breaking.

Daniel Stephens (12)
Mounts Bay School

THE BUZZARD

If you go out for a drive,
around the south coast of Cornwall
you might just see on top of a tree,
a fantastic fierce buzzard watching.

He's got big bulging eyes that stare,
and fine claws that can squash a hare.
With huge great wings that stretch a few metres
he then glides through the sky with ease.

He spots his prey on the ground,
it turns out to be a rabbit running.
He starts his descent from high in the sky,
then he swoops, his claws enwrapping.

It's a scare! He catches the rabbit,
and flies up to the top of the tree.
He starts to rip the red fresh flesh apart,
then he lets the carcass drop silently to the ground.

Alistair Sedgeman (12)
Mounts Bay School

HALLOWE'EN

Ghostly figures climbing on the walls,
Spooky footsteps and werewolf calls,
A chilling breeze, scary sounds,
I think I'll take a look around!
Monster growls from under my bed,
I think there's something on my head!
Snapping jaws from in the room,
I'll get up to meet my doom!
Down the hall where the goblins lay,
Tip-toe quietly before they awake!
Dancing fairies beneath my feet,
Come with me to 'Trick or Treat'!
A glowing pumpkin in my hand,
The scariest place in the land!
A giant stomps me with his foot,
A spooky house, let's take a look!
'Trick or Treat' we cry with joy,
Some sweets, some fruit or even a toy!
Girls and boys are having fun,
Ghastly ghouls coming, let's run!
Fun and games at Hallowe'en,
You wouldn't believe where I've been!

Sally Payne (12)
Mounts Bay School

Olympics

The Olympics have gone,
No more viewing on TV,
No more gold, no more silver,
Not even a bronze.

The Olympics have gone,
You can't watch the running
Or the swimming,
You can't even watch the boxing.

The Olympics have gone,
No more rowing,
Seeing the high skill and quality
As they row away.

The Olympics have gone,
No more pictures of Australia,
Goodbye Sydney Opera House,
No more scenes of the outback.

The Olympics were fun,
They should have run and run,
But now they have gone
We will just have to wait,

Hurry up 2004!

Jessica Davy-Thomas (12)
Mounts Bay School

Olympics 2000 - The End

Closing ceremony like the closing of a door,
Drums beating causing a vibration on the floor.

Five rings starting to fade away from sight,
Last punch being thrown at the end of the fight.

Last point being scored in the net,
Happy people collecting their money from the bet.

Fireworks popping and banging in the sky,
Sad and happy faces as people wave goodbye.

Cara Beeley (13)
Mounts Bay School

Olympic Poem

Jonathan Edwards and Steve Redgrave,
are both Olympic champions,
Steve is one amazing rower,
and so are his companions.
Jonny flew an amazing length,
with his power and tremendous strength.

Audley Harrison and Steve Backley,
are other Olympic champions,
Audley got the gold for Britain,
and made many more companions.
Steve Backley is the king of throwing,
but the event that impressed me was rowing.

Aidan Moffatt (13)
Mounts Bay School

FIREWORKS

The Olympics are over,
It's time to celebrate,
Fireworks are about to break.
They screech like cats,
Bang like balloons,
Sparkle like diamonds in the sky,
The crowd cheer,
People clap,
Everyone's got a can of beer to tap!

Tim Lewis (13)
Mounts Bay School

TRIUMPH

I couldn't believe it,
I was finally here,
With my adrenaline rushing,
And the roaring crowds cheer,

My enemies fighting,
They were up to the test,
Each one brilliant,
I was up next.

My memories flooded back,
All the blood and gore,
All the javelin training,
This is what it was for.

But now it was time,
To show what I could do,
To be the very best,
Could I pull it through?

Up I went,
The pole firmly in my grasp,
My knuckles clenched white,
To fulfil my task.

The whistle went,
And into action I sprang,
The pole flew out of my hands,
My part was done.

Was I the winner?
Had I achieved my dream?
Emotions were everywhere,
The winner, was me!

Lindsey Nicholls (13)
Mounts Bay School

WEMBLEY

Wembley's famous turf is being destroyed
To make way for a new birth
All the history will crumble
When the Twin Towers fall
World Cups, Olympic Games,
Domestic cups, European Championships
And even pop concerts!
Gone, forever
World Cup 1966
Those famous words
Geoff Hurst, Bobby Moore, Gordon Banks
Bringing the glory back to England
Will Wembley's past haunt its future?

Tim Williams (12)
Mounts Bay School

OLYMPICS

Bang went the gun,
The race had begun,
Running as fast as a bullet,
One hundred metres to go,
As fast as it's ever been run.

Cameras flashing, clocks must be crashing,
Looking at the time that's been run,
One hundred metres have been run,
And inside world record pace,
I've run the race,
Won the race,
Coming in gold medal place.

The race was run,
The race was won,
The spectators had lots of fun,

The 2000 Olympics have finished,
Now it's Athens 2004.

John Rule (12)
Mounts Bay School

My Home

My home is Cornwall
For holidaymakers it's heaven.
They don't like it at all
When it rains six days out of seven.

My home is Cornwall
Where there are fields all around.
You can play catch or football
And campsites abound.

My home is Cornwall
Where the coast path follows the sea.
You'll see many different types of gull
And places selling a cream tea.

My home is Cornwall
Rugged coves and sandy bays.
It's beautiful at any time
Bring your surfboard and catch some waves.

My home is Cornwall
I'm glad that I live here.
The visitors have to go home
And some will shed a tear.

Greg Lever (12)
Mounts Bay School

OLYMPIC 2000!

To start the Games comes
the Olympic torch,
it doesn't just come from
someone's back porch.

All the words that have
been spoken,
are like the records that
have been broken.

In the pool or on the track
you know the Olympics will
come back!

Lauren Oats (12)
Mounts Bay School

WEIGHT LIFTER

Chalk up,
The fire inside is burning,
Bend down, the power is ready to blast,
The strong oak tree takes its stance,
Push,
He is competing,
Tick-tock, tick-tock,
Till he has dropped,
It's a new record!

Nathan Oliver (13)
Mounts Bay School

GYMNASTICS - OLYMPICS

Girls get ready in their glittery costumes,
Girls sparkle while they move in position,
You can sense the tension,
People wait in anticipation,
Jump, flick and twist in the air
Like a shooting star.
Still jumping, turning high into the sky.

Melissa Phillips (13)
Mounts Bay School

100m Sprint

Focused is the sprinter,
Like a lion ready to pounce,
And they're off.
Tearing like a tiger through the forest,
Bolting like a cheetah across the desert plane,
Only two others separate him from gold
He speeds up, like a black panther on the chase
And over the line . . . He's won
Like a tiger that's caught his prey.
The crowd cheer, like the lion's loud roar of dominance.
The Olympics are over and the crowd no longer cheer but,
All the great Olympic heroes
Will all be back in the next four years.

Luke Howes (13)
Mounts Bay School

SYDNEY 2000

I'm on the track I'm ready to go
If I don't start soon I'm gonna blow,
I feel the urge to just run and run
I'm waiting for the bang of the gun.

Bang! That's the gun we all start racing
As I run my mind is pacing,
I feel such adrenaline the heat is on
You look in front and then I'm gone.

I'm coming first I'm gonna win
The chances of catching are very thin,
I'm seconds away from my victory
Time to show those who doubted me.

The rush, the feeling, the anticipation
The need to win, the determination,
The line is near, the gold is mine
The passion I feel, this is my time,

I've scored my goal, I've won my pride,
If only you knew what I'm feeling inside,
You're all here to witness my wrath
Time to show you who had the last laugh.

Jamie Tobin (15)
Mounts Bay School

OLYMPICS 2000

Good day and welcome
To the Olympics 2000

See running, rowing
Swimming and throwing

Jonathan Edwards on his last jump
Now hear the chanting from the crowd

Can he win gold?
To make our country feel bold

Off he goes hop, skip, jump
Oh no! He's forgotten his asthma pump

Yes, he's up in the air
Flying without a care

He lands, a personal best
Now he needs a good earned rest

He's won the gold
And grips it with a tight firm hold

We thank him for winning
So we all can start singing

We've really had a lot of fun
That's it from Sydney in the sun.

Scott Harvey (11)
Mounts Bay School

Ducking And Diving

He danced around the ring
Ducking and diving
Determined to be the king
Ducking and diving
The heavyweight title calls
Ducking and diving
His opponent takes the fall
Ducking and diving
From the boxer's dynamite hand
Ducking and diving
The punches start to land
Ducking and diving
His emotions seem so cold
Ducking and diving
Determined to win the gold
Ducking and diving
The bell rings out loud
Ducking and diving
The noise is growing in the crowd
Ducking and diving
His name is Audley Harrison
Ducking and diving
He becomes Olympic Champion
Ducking and diving.

Matthew Brown (15)
Mounts Bay School

OLYMPIC POEM

O lympics were here and they were great
L ots of athletes came to compete.
Y ears of practice these athletes have put in
M ay pay off at these Olympics.
P lenty of records were broken
I n the track and field events
C losing ceremony with fireworks and fun
S ydney 2000, the modern Olympics are done.

Ross Williams (12)
Mounts Bay School

THE RACE IS ABOUT TO START!

On your marks . . .
Set . . .
Bang! . . .
Heart thumping . . .
Muscles aching . . .
Breathing's getting harder . . .
Nearly there . . .
10 more metres . . .
Finish line ahead . . .
It's very close . . .
I dip my head . . .
Hooray! I've won the gold!

Clare Noall (13)
Mounts Bay School

RUNNING

Running is a sport which pushes you to your hardest.
If you're running a long distance and you're tired, sore
and aching, you must keep at it to be a medallist.
You must finish wherever you're coming.
Push yourself to the limit and just keep running.
Before the race, nervous, thinking that I've got to be
number one, can't be number two.
Out to beat the world record, my personal too.
Bang! We're off.
I got around the second bend.
Tired already, must keep running until the end.
The bell rang! Last four hundred metres, one more lap to go.
He was gaining a bigger lead, oh no!
Coming up to two hundred metres left, must win gold.
I went as fast as my legs could carry me, I'm aching,
panting, tired and sore all over.
Suddenly he began to slow down, his legs must be aching and old.
Yes, I'm ahead.
But he's coming back and he's really putting it in now.
We finish, it must be close, I didn't know whether to be
happy or be sad and whine.
Then it was announced, I had won by a head, the gold was mine.

Matthew Howes (13)
Mounts Bay School

My First Event

The crowd is cheering,
The sun crackles through the clouds,
Broken shadows trek across the stadium,
I step up for my first event - running,
'On your marks, get set . . .'
Blood is pumping through me,
A rush of adrenaline catches up with me
And I almost topple over.
'Bang!'
We are off, racing one another, wanting
To win for our country.
The ground jumps up and down, wobbles
Under my feet,
The sun escapes the clouds, almost blinding me.
The rush of the wind against me,
Threatens to push me back to the start,
The finish line is getting ever more closer,
Pouncing upon me like a lion pouncing on its prey,
And before I know it, it's all over,
I do not know if I've won or lost,
It does not matter,
I'm proud to have run for my country,
I hope my country is proud of me for doing my best.

Lisa Olds (14)
Mounts Bay School

THE OLYMPICS

First day of Olympics dawns,
The sun rises, casting shadows,
Rollers break on the beach.
A warm breeze makes the flags flutter,
Creating the colours of a carnival.
As the crowd fill the stadium,
Adrenaline makes the air suffocating.
As mid-day draws near, the heat rises
Along with the excitement,
The athletes and crowd stand filled with tension.
As the day draws to a close
The crowd trickle home and spend a sleepless night waiting
For the next thrilling day.

Jennifer Rule (14)
Mounts Bay School

CITIUS, ALTIUS, FORTIUS

The Olympics, people come from far and wide,
Balloons, streamers, cheering, people sitting on every side,
The games begin, the athletes get tense,
The starters are ready, you can feel the suspense,
Gymnastics, diving, running and more,
Everyone looks up to see their teams score,
Great Britain are cheering, the nation's in bliss,
Years since we've competed better than this,
The curtain comes down leaving Aussie in peace,
Another four years we'll be in Greece.

Holly Hobson (14)
Mounts Bay School

OLYMPICS - SYDNEY 2000

Four years of hard work,
Lap after lap,
Length after length,
All put to the test in a few minutes of glory . . . or sorrow.

All the hype built up by the media,
Predictions made,
Bets placed,
Britain's medal hopefuls, the pride of the nation.

The Olympic spirit displayed brilliantly,
'Eric the swimmer,'
Swimming the 200m,
That's what these games are all about.

But for all of this, there's one downside,
Drug scandals,
Cheating nations,
They're only winners on paper.

The best British Olympics since 1924,
Eleven gold,
Twelve silver,
Now it's back to training until Athens.

Jamie Gill (14)
Mounts Bay School

THE OLYMPICS

Four long years of training hard,
But finally you've made it here,
The challenge has been tough for all,
But your strong will has carried you here.

From different countries athletes have met,
Brought together to fight to be the best,
In opposite activities people may excel,
But only one will achieve what everyone dreams of.

Sydney 2000, the best there has been,
It was your dedication which took you there,
To compete, challenge and reach your goal,
You may not have come first but you are
Still a winner!

Emma Thomas (14)
Mounts Bay School

THE OLYMPICS

O nly four years training just for a few days of glory
L aps and laps of the track just for one round disc of metal.
Y elling crowds cheering for their country to win,
M illions of people watching it all over the world.
P layers from around the globe, competing for their country.
I ntense competition for world records, let alone winning.
C elebrations at the opening and closing ceremonies.
S candalous goings on with cheats and drugs.

Martin Packford (14)
Mounts Bay School

My Thing!

I went down to the Olympics,
To try my hand at sport
I'd watch all the brilliant professionals,
And then do it myself (I thought).

First, I tried the cycling,
And saw Quealey get us first place,
So I went down to the race track
To see the opponents I'd face,
But my brakes got stuck before we began
And I never started the race
(I decided cycling wasn't my thing!)

Then I went down to the swimming
The swimmers were really first rate,
So I got changed and stepped outside
But my armbands wouldn't inflate!
(I decided swimming wasn't my thing!)

I thought I'd try the sprinting next,
So I made my way to the track,
I knelt down and prepared myself
And was glad we weren't against the clock,
But when the gun fired, I couldn't get up,
My foot had got stuck on the starting block.
(I decided sprinting wasn't my thing!)

I had enjoyed my Olympics,
Even though I hadn't quite got gold
I'd decided to watch the pros do their stuff
And then in Athens, I was sure
That all my dreams would unfold.

Lydia Williams (14)
Mounts Bay School

Olympic Poem

A salty tear ran down her cheek
as she stepped up to the stand,
a gold medal round her neck
and flowers in her hand.

She looked so proud to be flying her flag
around the race track,
feeling on top of the world
she didn't look back.

Then came the national anthem
where she sung her heart out
because she'd won for her country,
she's a hero there's no doubt.

She went home knowing
she'd fulfilled her dream.
Will she be back for the next Olympics?
Yes, we heard her scream!

Jennifer Lawry (14)
Mounts Bay School

SYDNEY

Joining in the stadium
The crowd shouts and cheers
Stars come out of the corners
Climbing onto platforms,
Waving to the crowd.

People of all ages
Perform what they've rehearsed
Creating a great atmosphere
And lots of happy smiles
Keeping people cheery.

The athletes join together
To show they are good sports
Listening and joining in the fun
Before the events begin.

The torch is ignited
And the stadium glows.
The games have begun
And the whole world knows
They must work for their dreams
And reach for their goals.

A world united by a single desire
The Olympic goal:
'Faster, stronger and higher'.

Jennifer Gee (14)
Mounts Bay School

ROWING - COXLESS FOURS

As the whole nation watches their tele
All hoping that Steve Redgrave and his three team mates attempt to secure another gold medal for Great Britain,
With only a few countries even trying to challenge the unstoppable GB crew so their expectations are high.

All the crews from other countries including Great Britain line up at the start all fit and primed to go,
The starter blows his whistle and all the teams give a big push with their legs and hail their oars through the water with tremendous force and lightening quick speed,
The rowers now have to give their all for the next 100 metres,

As the teams come up to the last 250 metres, the rowers are still pushing and pulling like a flash on the oars,
With the finish line coming closer the rowers are making the strokes count, knowing that every ounce of power will count and separate the medalists to the losers,
On every rower's face there is an expression of grit and determination.

The British and the Italians are terribly close to each other,
Too close for a clear view of the winner,
All the British fans restlessly wait for the final result,
The whole nation is peering at the tele for the scoreboard and to observe the order,

1 Great Britain
2. Italy
3. Australia

Everybody suddenly jumps out of their seats and start celebrating, jumping up and down, and shouting like there is no care in the world,
Meanwhile the four British take a short rest in their boats, then Matthew Pinsent climbs over the man behind him to hug Steve Redgrave, congratulating him for his fifth Olympic gold medal, he then stumbles into the water, celebrating all the time.

The whole crew knows that all the time and effort they have put in, for the last four years has finally paid off.
When they got onto land all the other nations congratulate them for winning the gold medal,

All this went on at half past midnight, so I went to bed knowing that the Great Britain crew did the job for the team and for all the people at home.

Robert Corbett (14)
Mounts Bay School

Sydney 2000

The whistle blew, they took their marks,
Taking a deep breath, peering down the track at their ambition.
Crouching down they located their feet on the starting blocks.
The speaker sounded again, 'Set!'
Backs raised and heads lowered, they paused.
The starter hooted.
Almost immediately surges of power entered their legs.
The acceleration was phenomenal.
As they hurtled down the track their heads were raised.
All men on tip-toes almost mimicking a cheetah.
Arms were tense, pulling the air behind them.
Now closer to the finish line a leader was emerging.
They dipped for the line like a fleeing ostrich.
The winner peered at the notice board
Arms raised, saluting the crowd.
All congratulated each other,
Shaking hands and hugging.

The winner did a lap of honour,
His perseverance had paid of,
Gold at last!

Aran Jackson (14)
Mounts Bay School

Sydney 2000

Ready, steady go!
Britain are off,
They're in the lead,
Can they stay there.
Yes, they can!
Redgrave does it again.

It's not about winning or losing,
It's about representing your country,
Sometimes you make it
Sometimes you don't,
All we want is their best.

My smile grows bigger,
When I hear the words,
'Britain are the Olympic gold medalists.'
So come on lads,
Do it for your country.

Sydney 2000,
What an event,
A glamorous start
And a sensational finish,
Some dreams are achieved
And some are demolished.

Matthew Gendall (14)
Mounts Bay School

OLYMPIC POEM

The Sydney Olympics were on the way,
Morris Green is out to play,
Michael Johnson, Marrion Jones,
The winners of their race have got their gold.

Audley Harrison brings back Britain,
Cathy Freeman's aboriginal sprinting,
Steve Redgrave, Olympiad's dream,
While Colin Jackson fails the team.

Richard Laity (14)
Mounts Bay School

OLYMPIC POEM

The gun fired,
As the athletes shot off,
Focused and concentrated
They sped into the distance of the track.

The scream of excitement
Buzzing through the crowd
Deafening and screeching
Roaring so loud.

Desperately wanting to win,
Sweating with determination,
They strain to the finish,
And salute their nations.

The athletes relax,
And try to recover,
Most are happy,
And glad it's over.

Remy Dickson (14)
Mounts Bay School

SYDNEY 2000

The Olympics had so many games.
People came from far and wide
To watch and compete.
The gymnasts elegantly did their moves.
Twisting and turning in all directions.

Crowds gathered to watch the events and cheer
On their countries.
Roaring with excitement.
The athletes are trying to win as many medals as possible.

The swimmers gliding through the water.
Slashing as if their arms were blades.
Tension builds, as they become closer to the blue tiled wall.
Who will touch it first?
One big splash and the athlete emerges from the water.
Arms raised highly above their head.
Fists clenched tightly.
The crowds cheer.
We have a winner.

Many other games went on at Sydney.
At the end of it all one spectacular ceremony.
Parades and famous people walked and danced around.
To finish it off loads of fireworks and one huge party.
Everyone happy and now ready to go home.

Sophie Rogers (14)
Mounts Bay School

OLYMPICS

O pening ceremony,
L eaping long jump,
Y achting is fun but hard,
M ulti-athletes need all fitness,
P lenty of hard work,
I ndividual people,
C oming together,
S o they can compete together.

Sophie Atkins (13)
Mounts Bay School

GOING FOR GOLD

Jonathan Edwards was going for gold,
His heart and soul he had sold,
A nation's hopes and dreams he held,
'I'll clear the pit!' he screamed and yelled.

He took a breath and found his mark,
Digging deep for that extra spark,
He ran like the wind and flew like a bird,
The delight of the crowd, their voices he heard.

He knew he had done it, the *gold* was his,
No silver, no bronze, the *gold* was his,
A nation's pride, a nation's joy,
For Britain's jumping golden boy.

Ian Tucker (13)
Mounts Bay School

Olympics

All the participants prepare to run,
Giving their ready signal one by one,
Eight different men up against the line,
It's time to begin the race against time.

Puffing and panting as they speed down the track,
Focusing forward, never looking back,
Hearts pounding like a constant drum beat
Cheering blending with the tapping of their feet.

Like a herd of elephants they thunder on,
The start line has long behind them gone,
With only 300 metres to go,
It started to form a memorable show.

The sprinters started to separate up,
But only one person could win the gold cup,
As all the contestants crossed the line,
It was said that Britain broke the world record time.

Penny James (15)
Mounts Bay School

DESTINATION SYDNEY

From the strongest to the weakest,
USA to Equatorial New Guinea,
Maurice to Eric,
Everyone united to celebrate.

This was the two weeks
That athletes had been training for
During the last four long years,
Was this to be their time?

The quickest by far was Greene,
He was as fast as a cheetah,
With a distinctive swagger,
And personality to match.

The slowest was Eric the Eel,
He was as slow as a snail,
Yet everyone supported him,
Showing the true Olympic spirit.

Now another four years
Until it returns to its birthplace,
The XXVIII Olympiad,
2004 is destination Athens.

Tracy Attridge (15)
Mounts Bay School

OLYMPIC POEM

Running, swimming, jumping, arms like rock,
Excited people watching,
It's time against the clock.

Can he do it, yes he can,
Legs and arms get tired,
Past the winning line he goes,
It's gold for England
His heart is on fire.

Matthew Francis (14)
Mounts Bay School

The Olympics

People entering Sydney hoping their country will win,
The crowd goes silent as the first race is about to begin,
'On your marks, get set, go!'
USA comes first, the other countries call out,
'Oh no!'
Next it's the hurdles, Colin Jackson lines up.

Let's hope he comes through,
If he doesn't win then I'll expect the whole of Britain
will be saying,
'What shall we do?'
He comes to the finish line, the last bit of the straight
He's coming up, he wins first place as the other teams
come in two minutes late.

The final race . . .
All the other teams are thinking, trying to set their pace,
The pressure's on Britain if they want to win gold.
Great Britain, they've done it, they were so bold.

Maree Smith (13)
Mounts Bay School

The Olympics

After travelling thousands of miles,
From Athens to Sydney, by land and sea,
Passed from hand to hand the Olympic torch arrives,
The fifth of September and the Sydney Harbour Bridge
Launches its dazzling complexion of fireworks,
At that moment the giant torch begins its spectacular
Two week blazing dance,
People stand awe-struck as the city stains a thousand colours.

The morning after and it all begins,
Everyone's ready and all prepared,
They wait for the gun . . . *bang,*
The runners run, the swimmers swim,
The rowers row, the shooters shoot,
The jumpers jump, the throwers throw.

For two weeks they battle it out,
Until at last it's all over,
At the final ceremony again the fireworks are launched,
This time they do not stain the city but wash away the marks,
As the last minutes approach the torch runs low,
Until the last flicker of their dance sleeps for another four years.

Harry Penhaul (14)
Mounts Bay School

FLICKERING FLAME

Set fire to the torch,
That burns bright
All day and all night,
An orange flame,
A yellow flame,
Flickering, flickering,
Warmth floods over you
It warms you right through.

Natalie Mitchell (11)
Mounts Bay School

Sunset Lion

For there is a lion that sits in the sun
Bathes in the moon before the day has begun
        For there is a lion who hunts for his prey
And sits in the streams of the sun's beautiful ray
        For there is a lion no more he shall be
. . . For hunter is searching, searching for thee.

Karina Fleming (12)
Mounts Bay School

THE OLYMPIC GAMES

The Olympic Games is a marvellous event,
From rowing to running, boxing to throwing.

The athletes wear all kinds of clothes from
Crocodile shorts to kangaroo shirts.

It must be truly amazing to be up there
On the podium listening to your national anthem
Being played to all the world with a beautiful
Gold medal around your neck.

The closing ceremony was as good as the
Opening ceremony.
The Olympics were brilliant and entertaining
From the start to the finish.

Thomas Bodinar (11)
Mounts Bay School

I'm In The Olympics

Yes, I'm going in the Olympic games.
Winning a gold medal is my aim.
Swimming, running all those things,
When I look up people start to sing.
Getting into all our gear
Look a kangaroo that's very near.
Koalas, dingo, platypus in all,
There's a kangaroo that's very tall.
Now let's get on the running track,
Let's hope that koala hasn't a six pack.
Running and jumping, lots to see,
Oh look those animals are cheering for me!
I'm ahead of every other.
I'm now looking at my mother.
I'm on my balcony,
People still cheering for me.
I won the gold medal, yes,
And watch a kookaburra reaching its nest.
Closing ceremony is at an end.
Let's hope I don't go round the bend.

Jodi Hughes (11)
Mounts Bay School

Olympics

The England team stepped off the plane
Their goals have been fulfilled
Gold, silver and bronze medals around their necks
The fans cheering wildly.

Missing the weather back in Sydney
Memories coming back
Steve Redgrave smiles for cameras
Denise Lewis says words for newspapers.

Looking back on their victories
Setting sights for four years time
A sense of achievement fills the air
Proud to represent the country.

Remembering the animals, talents and events
Platypus, koala and kangaroo
Athletics, gymnastics, water sports too,
The motivation, determination and the training.

Thinking back to the sound of the start gun
The fans shouting at the sides
The national anthem playing loudly
Sport stars have been created.

It's been 70 years since we've had such success
Why would anyone feel disappointed?
In four years time we'll try again
And maybe do even better!

Zoe Roberts (12)
Mounts Bay School

THE OLYMPIC MEDALS

M agnificently good
E xciting honour
D etermination to win
A mazing, fascinating
L ucky to win one
S uper to get one.

Jamie Jacka (12)
Mounts Bay School

THE OLYMPICS 2000

Olympics happen every four years,
Long jump, javelin and many more
Years came by very slowly,
But when the time comes it's worth waiting for.

People win medals sometimes gold, silver and bronze,
And at the closing ceremony people sing different songs
My favourite events are gymnastics and swimming
And you see them always jumping and diving!

Lisa Moyle (11)
Mounts Bay School

My Family

First there's my dad
And when he's afraid
He goes out of the house
And hides like a mouse.

Of course there's my mum
She likes to drink rum
She is the boss
And doesn't like a lot of fuss.

Then there's my sister
She likes to bicker
She likes to play football
And says I'm not cool.

Then there's me
My name is Lee
I like to read and
And I am told I'm happy and bright.

Lee Collins (11)
Mounts Bay School

Australian Animals

Australia is the place to be,
Kangaroos, koalas, there's loads to see,
There's a little joey with mummy Roo,
Don't forget the platypus and the dingo too.
There are kookaburras and a wallaby,
Looking so wild and free.

Megan Hipson (11)
Mounts Bay School

The Special Event

The Olympics is a special event
The greatest games God ever sent,
I look forward to every four years
To see the athletes (sometimes in tears).

People come to fulfill their dream
And hope they've got the perfect team.
The best medal to win is gold
Which would never ever be sold.

The closing ceremony is just great
And I hope that I'm never late
To hear them sing their song
And often sing along.

Kayleigh Cheel (11)
Mounts Bay School

THE OLYMPICS

The Olympics started with the Greeks
Every four years now, over several weeks
Each country send their best athlete
To compete for gold - no mean feat!

Runners, swimmers, hockey players too
So many sports, too many to go through
Like a performance, it's great to see
You really are hooked by week three!

As well as success, there's also tears
Through injuries, mishaps - all of their fears
Records get broken all the time
And if there are cheats - what a crime.

Thousands of people tune in each day
And thousands more go there to stay
To watch the events as they unfold
The Olympics - a sight to behold.

Jacob Travers (11)
Mounts Bay School

OLYMPICS

Olympics only comes every four years
Loving it when you're out there
Your own country's team you're in
Many different kinds of sports
People watching you from all over the world
In the stadium after you've won
Cyclists round the stadium, tired out, but
Supporting our country.

Chris Tonkin (11)
Mounts Bay School

OLYMPICS

Opening the Olympics with a flaming torch,
Lots of people watching the Olympic Games,
Yachts were racing on the blue sea,
Medals were won: gold, silver and bronze,
People having a wonderful time,
Improving by every second, the runners go by,
Centre of attraction as I win my gold medal,
Splendid, the fireworks start, it's the end of the Olympics.

Nathan Firth (11)
Mounts Bay School

OLYMPICS

The Olympics were an amazing sight,
With the flame and rings shining very bright.
Jonathan Edwards jumped big and bold,
Which won him the best, that shining gold.
Steve Redgrave got his five,
And I'm surprised that he's still alive!

Will anyone ever beat Maurice Green?
He's big, he's bad and very mean!
The Americans are just so good
They all live in their own neighbourhood!
Marion Jones, she's as quick as lightning,
And for a girl that's very frightening!

The Americans are just the best,
They always come out better than the rest,
The closing ceremony went off with a bang,
As for the singers, they just sang,
The flame went out that night,
But we still had the fireworks
Which were very bright!

Damon Nicholls (12)
Mounts Bay School

THE LONG JUMP

The deafening crack of the gun as it fires.
I'm running down the bouncy tarmac track,
My speed increasing every second,
Approaching the dusty sand pit,
Glancing at my audience cheering for me,
My legs working harder and harder.

I leap through the air,
My heart pounding so fast I can't control it,
I land with a massive loud thud,
Sand all over my sweaty face as if it was dust,
I rise to my feet,
My audience clapping with delight,
I now think,
That was it.

Claire Allen (11)
Mounts Bay School

OLYMPIC DREAM

The atmosphere is electric,
The human line is tense,
They wait to start.

Bang goes the gun,
They're all chasing each other,
Run, run, run.

Leap, jump, throw,
They're all going for gold,
Go, go, go.

Bronze, silver, gold,
Young and old,
They're all trying their best,
It's the ultimate test.

All different colours, race and size,
They all come together for the ultimate prize.

Amy Willcox (11)
Mounts Bay School

Pole Vault

Running down the runway with a massive pole,
Digging it into the ground, I hope I find the hole,
Pulling me up and over, I hope I miss the bar,
Flying through the air and landing horribly hard.

I got up all excited, the crowd were cheering on,
They really pushed me on to become a champion.

Ashley Pearce (11)
Mounts Bay School

Hopes And Dreams

Bang goes the gun,
The race has now begun,
Hearts are beating, thump, thump,
Keep on going, legs pump,
Legs are aching, push on,
You weren't fast enough, medals gone.

Psyching yourself before the jump
The horse before knocked the bar with a thump,
Your go now, you're cantering up fast
Leap your highest, that's heat one passed,
You clear the rest, your pace is bold
No more faults, you win the gold.

Taking part is the name of the game,
But winning medals will bring you fame,
Redgrave, Pincent, Lewis and Harrison,
All achieved their life-long ambition,
The Olympic flame will never cease,
We will see it again when it burns in Greece.

Lucy Brown (11)
Mounts Bay School

LEAPING FOR GOLD

Leaping far, leaping for gold,
The blustering wind cool and cold,
As I leap through the air,
I think in my mind shall I dare.

The crowd watch and go quiet,
If I don't win there will be a riot,
I see the spot where I want to land
I hurl myself to the ground.

I look to the scoreboard, how have I done,
I stare to the crowd and see my mum,
Everything goes silent and still
My face so serious, I'm out to kill.

I've won it I just know in my mind
My scores come up, it seems I'm blind,
You've won it I was told,
Yes, I've done it, I've won the *gold*.

Chloe Matthews (12)
Mounts Bay School

OLYMPIC RUNNER

Four years to go, already training well
The nerves and pressure are so immense
Every season running, only time will tell.
Three years to go, legs are getting strong,
Always training, every day, winter days are long.
Two years to go, entering all events.
Long days of training, wearing out my shoes.
One year to go, now I must not lose.
Gun fires, flying through the air, everybody goes.
Pounding heart, past the runners, am I the winner, who knows?

Bryony Jelbert (11)
Mounts Bay School

Dreams Come True

As I stepped up to the weights
With confidence and determination
And as I starts to bend down to lift the weights
The silence begins.

Gradually all the pain and agony starts
With all the back breaking work,
It's all paid off,
I've won gold!

Robert Heath (11)
Mounts Bay School

Dive!

Nerves,
As I walked slowly and carefully towards
The springboard, my feet making a
Slap, slap, slap.

Excitement,
As I prepare to jump into the warming water of relief.

Pride,
As I proudly stretch high, pushing out my chest.

Adrenaline,
As I leap into the air and twist myself around into a triple turn
All I can hear is the whistling of the wind rushing through my ears,
The crowd roaring endlessly. Plunging downwards, heading for
Imaginary target painted in the ripples.

Relief
As I fall head first into the reassuring calm waters.

William Johns (12)
Mounts Bay School

SWIMMING WINNER

Bang! Goes the gun,
The crowd are silent,
Splash! Go the swimmers,
As they all dive in.

The crowd are now shouting,
As loud as a fire bell.

The swimmers coloured hats bobbing up and down,
And arms coming in and out the water,
Their legs kicking very hard,
Making very big splashes.

As they get to the last length of the race,
The crowd are going wild,
The end didn't seem very far away to us
But to them I bet it seemed miles.

As the first person touched the end,
The crowd stood up and cheered,
The winner raised his arms,
Looking very pleased with himself,
He shouted, 'Winner.'

Then at the very end the shiny gold
Medal got placed around his neck.

Kimberly Knott (11)
Mounts Bay School

Olympic Rowing

Holding on to my oars,
Waiting for the start gun.
Heart pounding.
Suddenly like a roar of a lion
The start gun, *bang!*
The crowd roar and scream as we take off.

We are pulling, pushing, pulling, pushing,
Moving faster every stroke,
Arms straining, hurting.

Keep moving, half way
Second now, gliding along the water,
Catching the opponents, not much further.
Eyes blurring, just see the finish line,
We are drawing now.

10 metres, 9, 8, 7 arms bursting,
6, 5, 4, 3 overtaking, 2, 1, 0.
We won!
We are so happy in pain
But we won.

Ross Lawrence (11)
Mounts Bay School

IT'S UP TO YOU!

Our hearts were in our mouths
As one last horse galloped into the ring.
The silver medal was at stake.

The crowd was screaming
A sudden fall of noise hit the arena
At last the bell had gone.

Over the first jump, 2nd, 3rd and 4th,
Higher and higher, faster and faster,
Wider and wider, on she goes.

The final jump was looming,
The crowd was roaring and clapping,
Would she make it with 5 seconds to go.

The English flags were flying
She made it with a clear round
The silver medal was ours.

Lauren Corbett (12)
Mounts Bay School

SYDNEY OLYMPICS

Sydney Olympics, 2000 is the year,
Gun shots, world records, loud shouting and cheers.

Determination, pride, an atmosphere you can feel,
Gold, silver, bronze and 'Eric the Eel.'

Long jump, high jump, tennis and swimming,
Gymnastics, discus, taking part and winning.

The day 'down under', heroes galore,
Steve Redgrave's fifth medal, who could ask for more.

Different countries and races all joined together
The Olympic torch may it burn forever.

Darren Jones (14)
Mounts Bay School

CHILDREN

C hildren playing in the park
H iding behind the trees
I saw a lot of people
L aughing, joking at me
D iving onto the grass
R acing up and down the track
E njoying myself
N ot too late to play another game.

Jamie Hill (11)
Mounts Bay School

2000 Sydney Olympics

The Olympics happens every four years,
Everyday the display becomes near.
Catherine Freeman is proud to be an Aborigine!
Great Britain did exceptionally well this year.

Running, jumping, javelin and swimming
Every person has a talent,
'Win, win, win! Bellowed the crowd,
'This Olympics is held in Sydney town!'

Americans take the lead again
We were lucky there was no rain
People coming, people going,
Britain's won medals in rowing!

Blue, black, red, yellow and green,
These are our Olympic teams
Two weeks and finally finished,
Just another four years until we compete again!

Floella Grosvenor (11)
Mounts Bay School

OLYMPICS 2000

Crowds are roaring,
High jumpers soaring,
Olympic torch burning,
Sporting events like
Football and sprinting,
Hurdles, jumping and more.
People stood on the
Podium screaming with joy.

James Buckland (11)
Mounts Bay School

Olympics 2000

Walking to the podium
Fans cheering me loudly,
Getting the gold medal
Listening to anthem proudly.

Starting to feel the emotions,
At the Olympics in Sydney,
Winning my first gold medal
Gran watching it on TV.

Going for my second gold,
In the running race,
People charging from behind,
So I started to pick up the pace.

Smashed the new world record,
I could see the coach's tears
Got another gold
Back in another four years.

Thomas Welch (11)
Mounts Bay School

GOING FOR GOLD

She is like a cheetah ready to pounce,
Gearing up for the race ahead.
She is as fast as a tiger.
As steady as a boulder buried in the deep blue sea.
She is a hover plane gently gliding over the track.
She is as strong as an ox, her legs strong as steel.
She carries on like a continuous journey, never stopping,
Never slowing until she gets to her destination.
She is an eagle swooping around the corners,
Searching for somewhere to land,
As she spots her goal anticipation fills her face.
As she finishes the race a wide smile glides over her face.

Hannah Richards (13)
Mounts Bay School

HURT SPIDERWEBS

Feeling the cold,
Any real love plummeting away from me
Left to rot or die.
Whichever occurs first.
Trapped in your spider web.
Cornered and afraid
Like the insect,
Unsuspecting prey.
Except the difference,
I know I'm simply being led astray.
My candle wax
Almost disappearing.
Once that has gone,
I know you'll come again.
You hide in shadows,
Thinking no one can see you.
You lurk in crevices,
Waiting to take me away with you.
I want to be wanted,
Need to be needed,
This battle takes some of the pain away,
And leaves me with a thumping feeling.
It makes me hungry,
Nothing left now to do
But sit and wait,
Wait for you,
Or for more of this hate.

Fen Potts (13)
Mounts Bay School

ALONE

He stands on the cliff
The loner
No cares in the world
The wind whips round his worried face.

The wind whistles through cracks in the rocks
The loner
In it, his cares are blown away
He's a loner
His tattered clothes cling to his skin.

Night comes, and darkness envelopes him
The loner
His heart beat quickens
He's a loner
The silence provokes his frightened thoughts
Alone.

Ben Oldcorn (13)
Mounts Bay School

THE LISTENERS IN THE POISONED HOUSE

Moonlight gleaming on glass.
A dark desolate silhouette.
As phantoms veiled a mystical cry, a moaning mansion
poisoned the sky.
A dismal door did the traveller seek.
His own fear betraying him, slaying him slowly.
The stranger stepped towards the ivy-shadowed wall.
His horse in the darkness cropping the forest's lashed floor.
Little was the traveller told that coffins clutched him,
breaking his soul.
Why? The traveller thought did the house stand here,
Covered by a thickness of crying leaves, which often dropped a tear.
So lonely looked the crumbling stone,
Which sighed a faint 'eeh' in a misty tone.
He smote on the door so abandoned and dead,
'Is anybody there.' The stranger said.
But nobody answered from the cobweb-fringed bed.
Nothing stirred, for all had fled.
He was the only thing breathing the cold night air.
Only the eyes of spirits lay upon his dark brow stare.
The traveller came closer to the rotten door.
'Is there anybody there.' He roared.
He looked through the keyhole and what was it he saw?
A bloodshed angel lain limp on the floor.
The traveller cursed its rocky shore.
'May the devil be with you for evermore.'
The traveller left unto the town.
But his words, poisoned, staying, lingering.
'May the devil be with you for evermore.

Georgina Yates (13)
Mounts Bay School

YELLOW!

Yellow is the colour of a meadow full of sunflowers
Yellow is sunny, warm and bright.
Yellow brings happiness to everyone around it
Yellow is the colour I like.
Yellow is the colour of a ripe lemon that grows on a sunny warm day.
The sun warms up my life
What warms up yours?
Please, I'd like to know.

Kate Smith (12)
Mounts Bay School

Blue

Blue is a colour, a favourite of mine,
It's the colour that spirals around in my mind,
It's the colour that's on all four of my walls,
It's the colour of uniform they should have in all schools,
It's the colour I wear and it's the colour I see,
It's the colour that only suits me,
Blue is the colour that makes you sad
When red is the colour that makes you mad,
What's my favourite colour I'm asking you,
But you all know the answer,
The answer is blue.

Benjamin Osborne (12)
Mounts Bay School

Olympic Poem

Bang goes the gun,
Starting all the fun.

Breaststroke, backstroke, front crawl too,
Swimming in the water clear and blue.

High jump, long jump, javelin and shot,
Now all the athletes are tired and hot.

They're like cheetahs running around a track.
The one at the front is the leader of the pack.

There is hockey, hurdles, gymnastics and rowing.
The number of medals won is now growing.

There are gold ones, silver ones, bronze ones too.
All of them glistening, shiny and new.

There are two weeks of laughter and fun.
Lots of races and events to be won.

Laura McGarry (12)
Mounts Bay School

The Olympics

Gymnastics was my favourite event,
In front of the telly was where most of my time was spent,
With their jumps and their dances,
They were like monkeys swinging from branches.
As a matter of fact she is a tiger pouncing around the arena.
Who'll win we just don't know,
She might be thrown off balance by a great big blow.
Will they keep going with the flow?
Or will they decide that they just won't go?
Gold, silver, bronze, or maybe even none,
You want to know,
So you'll have to go or just you wait and see.

Kylie Hughes (12)
Mounts Bay School

HOCKEY MATCH

They line up, bums out, sticks down.
The referee starts the thundering game.
The whistle starts
Wooh, wooh
Slap bang
Bang slap
Ooh, ooh, ooh
Sweat
Drip, drop
Drop, drip
Yuck!
Here, here
Line up
Crack, bang, bing, bong.
Whoosh
Bang
Yes, yes
We won!
Wooa, Wooa

Claire Noble (12)
Mounts Bay School

THE OLYMPICS

The Olympic games all excitement and famous names
Including Maurice Greene he's a running machine.
Jonathan Edwards he can jump.
Denise Lewis she did five and looked so alive!

Reece Clive (12)
Mounts Bay School

ORANGE!

Orange is the colour of a tropical fish.
Orange is the colour of a china dish.
Orange is the colour of a fisherman's boat,
And also is the colour of Kenny's coat.
Orange is the colour of a tiger's stripes.
Orange is the colour you see after night.
Orange is the colour of mud and dirt,
And the colour of the Dutch footie shirt.

Ben Stains (12)
Mounts Bay School

OLYMPICS 2000

Olympics 2000 is the place to be,
Live music and races come and join me.
If you can't make it, watch Channel Two.
My dear quick before you need the loo,
Put the radio on or the TV
I would come and sit with you
But I'm in Sydney.
Can't you see, the Olympic crowd are crazy.
I'll see you in 2004,
Let the madness come again.

Annie Jenkins (12)
Mounts Bay School

SWIMMING!

On your marks get set *bang!*
They're off splashing their legs
Gliding through the water
Like a dolphin moving up and down.
Their heads kept well down
Only to rise when they need to breathe.
Arms move perfectly together
As do the legs when they flap up and down
Swimming like this they'll never drown.

Laura Rosewall (11)
Mounts Bay School

RED IS!

Red is Arsenal, Liverpool and Manchester United.
Red is roses blowing gently in the wind.
Red is the Mounts Bay rugby top
Red is fresh juicy cherries
Red is a cold red bull
Red is a warning!
Red is danger
Red is . . .

Adam Fletcher (11)
Mounts Bay School

The Whale Song

No one seems to understand, what is going wrong.
Why animals are suffering, when we are going strong.
So grab a seat, sit on down, it won't take very long.
To give you all the gruesome facts in the whale song.
It started many years ago, from a fire star.
The sea was clear, the air was fresh with not one single car.
Animals ruled throughout the world, blessed no armies war.
Enough was left, no greedy men, no poverty or poor.
The monsters of the sea though gentle brushed with calm,
Were the whales of the water though no creature could they harm.
Oh no, men landed evolved from ape, some good but some quite stale.
Brains and selfishness did not agree, and the system went and failed.
The whales sang their echo song, to worn their friends to sink
As others like the DoDo did not make the count.
Extinct!
Whales cry to this day which makes the water salty,
As they know that we are the cause of why this world is faulty,
And as they sing from day to dusk, for they're sure that it is wrong
That they have to sing out their regrets, in the whale song.

Ellen Waghorn (13)
Mounts Bay School

ON YOUR MARKS . . .

On your marks, get set, go.
Red, yellow, blue, green, tops
All worn by the runners.
Everyone is nervous,
Slight smiles on their faces.
'Get to your places please.'
My heart starts to beat faster,
It feels as though it's going to
Pump out of my chest.
'On your marks, '*Bang go!'*
Run, run, faster, faster.
I can see the finishing line.
My legs are hurting,
My arms aching,
I am nearly there . . .
Yes, yes I have done it!

First!

Thomas Moyle (11)
Mounts Bay School

THE BIG APPLE

Taxis roaring, mopeds swerving,
While standing there
It's too busy for me!

The shops are big
It's like a maze
It's still too busy for me!

Leah Leydon (11)
Mounts Bay School

RED

As red as my blood
As red as my football kit
As red as my pants that I wear on my head.
As red as Miss May's top that she wears every day.
As red as rosy cheeks that smile and blush
As red as a face crying with anger
As red as my heart pumping Red Bull around my body.

Just Red!

Jack Wing (12)
Mounts Bay School

RED

Red is the blood that pours from your knife pierced back.
Red is your shoes, new from the shops!
Red is the anger raging inside!
Red are the strained eyes from doing too much work!
Red is the hair colour of punk rocker called Spike!
Red is a bike gleaming so bright!
Red are the leaves in the autumn season!
Red are the bon bons flavoured and juicy!
Red is a slide waiting to be ridden on!

Kieran James Knight (11)
Mounts Bay School

Blue

Blue as the sea
Blue as the sky
Blue as the pupil of my eye.

Blue is a blue tit fluttering around,
Blue is a pair of jeans making an awful sound
Blue is a clear night's sky.

Blue is a shark prowling about,
Blue is a rhino with a great big snout,
Blue is the background of my school tie.

Blue is dark but also cheerful
Blue is the colour I desire
Blue is the shade I admire.

Matt Lodey (12)
Mounts Bay School

GREEN

Green is the grass
in a field.
Green is the plants
which we admire.
Green is the snot
up your nose.
Green is a traffic light
as we wave goodbye.
Green is nature
all around us,
it is also green pus.

Jacob Phillips (12)
Mounts Bay School

BLUE

A bluebird's eye,
can see blue just like you and I,
shades of blue
cover the land,
headlands and heather just as blue.

A teddy bear
a body grow,
a blue oar
help me row!

The great sky,
the brill sea,
surround everything
that we can see.

The beaming
line of blue,
in the bow
that won't tie.

Smarties,
bonbons,
soft mints too,
everything, just everything is
Blue!

Nadia Preston (11)
Mounts Bay School

BLUE

Blue's the colour of the sea
And the colour of my teddy.
The colour of the great sky
Which spreads around you and I.
The colour of a peacock's feather
And great hills filled with heather.
Small marbles roll around
All along the smooth ground.
Light blue is the colour for shiver
It's all
Blue.

Cher Lourens (11)
Mounts Bay School

Rowing

All the boats lined up to start.
The crowd are waiting tensely,
The rowers grab their oars,
5 . . . 4 . . . 3 . . . 2 . . . 1 . . .
And they're off . . .
Pull, pull.
Great Britain take the lead,
Italy are pulling forward,
Pull, pull,

The crowd chant,
Go Redgrave, go Redgrave go!
Great Britain take the lead again . . .
They reach the line . . .
Gold for Great Britain,
The crowd go wild for Great Britain.

Cheryl Robbens (11)
Mounts Bay School

Black

Black is a knight
Using all his might
Slaying a dragon with his sword.

Black as night
Better than white
Some colours make me bored.

Black is a secret agent
Who is always on the internet
Sometimes evens bets.

Black is a knight.

David Baldwin (10)
Mounts Bay School

Gold 2000

Gold is the sun
Gold is the World Cup
Held by the winning captain
Gold is the medal
Won in the Olympics
Gold is money like rich people have
Gold is success
Gold is cool.

Ricky Welch (11)
Mounts Bay School

BLUE

Blue is the colour of my friend's bike
And it's the colour of my teddy Spike.

Blue is the colour of my old RE book
The weather is blue on a winter's day
My next door neighbour is always cold,
Her name is May.

Blue is the sea
So is the sky
Over me when I say, 'Hi.'

Down by the river it is watery like glue
What's your favourite colour,
Is it blue?

Chris Howarth (11)
Mounts Bay School

WHITE!

What do you think of when you see white?
Do you think of snow or a frosty night.

When I think of white I think of a field
Covered in snow, like it's been sealed for
The cold winter's blow.

White is like a bright light so brilliant
Your eyes can't stand the sight.

White is cold, white is nice,
White in the end is like chicken
And fried rice.

Verity Rogers (11)
Mounts Bay School

Red Is My Favourite Colour

Red reminds me of all the good things I've done,
Hooray,
I've always believed in that same colour,
Red is brilliant,
I've always succeeded in red,
Everyone else likes different colours,
Red is mine,
Red delicious apples,
Red leaves falling in autumn.

Harry Jeffries (11)
Mounts Bay School

LILAC!

Lilac for wine,
Lilac for flowers,
Lilac for sky,
Lilac is everything and I can't deny.

T-shirts are lilac,
As well as the sky
Look!

The rainbow,
Reminds me of lilac,
And the snow,
In the sunshine,
Makes tints of lilac.

Alice Le Vine (11)
Mounts Bay School

BLUE

My favourite colour is blue,
Like the sky,
Like a wool in thy air, blue,
Blue is a happy colour,
Blue is my favourite.

Kelly Edwards (12)
Mounts Bay School

Yellow

Yellow is the daffodil,
With its golden rays.
Yellow is the sand,
On warm sunny days.
Yellow is the sunset,
Golden as it rests.
Yellow is the canary,
Brooding in her nest.
Yellow is the burning stars,
That twinkle in the night.
Yellow is the life force,
That turns our dark to light.

Sarah-Jayne Gribben (11)
Mounts Bay School

SILVER

Silver's the moon
Silver's the galaxy
Silver's the stars twinkling in the sky
Silver's gold, shiny and bright when it's shone in the sunlight
Silver's a wish
Silver's a robot
Silver's the medals on the medal stand
Silver's the pistol, shiny and loud
Silver's the hub caps on the wheels that go round
Silver's allow never less shiny
Silver's glasses
Silver's the sun glistening on the sea
And none like it except for me!

Sam Draper (11)
Mounts Bay School

A Dog's Life

Some have posh cars,
Big houses, big jobs.
How does a dog feel?
What does he want?
He wants to follow you,
He wants to talk to you.
He is a reject,
He is an orphan.
He greets you when you come home,
Or so you think!
He is begging you.
He wants to be you.
He dreams he is a business Man,
His girlfriend is a babe,
His S-Type Jag is his dream.
Walk in his footsteps,
How do you feel?

Danielle Barr (13)
Mounts Bay School

STEVE REDGRAVE

He is an athlete,
An amazing athlete,
But he's not human,
He is an amazing robot, but not unique,
He and another were built to do a certain job,
He is as strong as an ox,
When the two of them do their job, nobody beats them.
These two golden robots were so great, they made two more
to do the same job.
The masters showed them the ropes,
The four 'creatures' are as strong as twelve men
But they are not perfect.
The four of them do not have a cox,
You could almost say that they are a coxless four.

Daniel Bateman (13)
Mounts Bay School

An Olympic Skeet Shooter

Eagle-eyed hunter,
Fast as a cheetah,
Calm as a whale,
Power . . . that is his weapon.

Target is fast,
A finely tuned machine,
Accuracy is victory,
Steadiness helps.

Perfect as an owl,
Smooth as an albatross,
Having trained for years,
This is the moment . . .

Steps up to the plate,
Proud as a lion,
Cocks the gun, fires,
Target - destroyed.

Darryl James (13)
Mounts Bay School

Stadium, Olympic Poem

I've just been finished,
Everyone now flooding in,
I've heard this next fortnight is going to be special,
This will be due to the:

O lympics
L oads of different sports
Y oung and old members
M any years of hard work
P eople from all over the world
I n every sport possible
C razy, but fit
S port is their life.

This, is what I'll see,
I have front row tickets,
No one to sit in my way,
Just sit on my seats.

I'm the new stadium,
Ready and raring for life!

The next sixteen days are mine!

Hannah Tenbeth (13)
Mounts Bay School

The End

Worried people scuttled around nervously,
Like ants do with a dead queen,
The cars had gone,
The trains had stopped,
Soon the streets would be deserted.
Three hours later a tramp,
Drunk and somehow disconnected
From the impending catastrophe
Stumbled into the high noon light,
And in his alcohol induced trance
Noticed that something was missing.
He glanced around,
And grasped hold of reality,
All the people had gone,
He searched his mind,
Going through it with a sieve,
And remembered what was happening,
In shock he fell into the street,
And saw four men,
Four darkly dressed figures,
Standing thirty feet high,
Nobody knows what went through his mind,
Perhaps he thought they were gods,
Or the horsemen of the apocalypse,
But he fell to his knees,
And cried until doom came
The sky rumbled,
As if the entire atmosphere was cracking open
And then there was nothing.

Matthew Watts (13)
Mounts Bay School

Olympic Event Of A Lifetime

Hear the shouts of 'You can make it',
One struggling hope for glory and fame.
In the first place he will fit,
He knows if he wins, he'll never be the same again.

I've got the gold,
The best I'm told,
Yet, empty I feel,
Like a plate with no meal.

There's no escape, it's my destiny,
I'd give it back, if it could be,
It looks so nice, so shiny and bright,
You can have it, it would bring delight.

Lies are spread, all about me,
Lies make me not happy,
I didn't take steroids to win,
Everything living knows it's a sin.

To win is to wonder, what would be,
If I did not win, but lost for all to see,
I would look like a fool,
Like a swimmer, drowning in his own pool.

My journey will end,
Killed by a friend,
Jealous of me, of what I am, what I have become,
It ended sad, but began as fun.

Emma Richards (13)
Mounts Bay School

SYDNEY 2000: 110M HURDLES

Colin Jackson crouches at the start,
He's about to embark on a voyage for supremacy.
It's taken years to get this far,
He calmly collects his anticipation.
Adrenaline pumped ferociously,
3 . . . 2 . . . 1, the gun is blasted,
And he's off.
Slicing the air,
Sprinting, he's a cheetah,
His opponents are his prey.
He reaches the first hurdle,
Propels himself forward.
He is a kangaroo, bounding over fallen acacias.
Seamlessly, he lands
Like a tornado, he fiercely races onwards.
Edges into the lead.
It's another hurdle,
The approach is fast,
One leg swings over,
A split-second later, the trailer follows perfectly.
For a moment he's weightless.
Then his ankles absorb the impact.
His legs transform the power into speed.
Then he clears the last jump.
An opponent falls.
It's a fast final furlong.
Thrusting forward, he's Concorde,
Cruising at Mach 2.
On course for his best result . . .
Yes, he's won the gold!

Tom Potter (13)
Mounts Bay School

DENISE LEWIS

With great determination,
She takes her place,
She stands on the track,
To begin the race.
She waves at the crowd,
As her name is called out,
'Come on Denise,'
You can hear them all shout.
The shot of a pistol,
The race has begun,
All of the athletes start to run.
They pick up speed as they go,
All want to win,
Cannot go slow.
One lap left,
Then that's all,
Keep your back up straight and tall.
Not long left now,
Pick up speed,
Can you hold onto the lead?
One last leap and it's all told,
Denise Lewis has won the gold!

Laura Jewell (13)
Mounts Bay School

THE LAST MATCH

The last match at Wembley was tense,
Could England beat Germany's defence.
The crowd cheered for England to score,
Only the shots were poor.

Germany pushed forward then came the fate,
The free kick to Germany.
They took it, the ball flew through the air
Like a missile aiming at its target.

Seaman moved too late, the ball brushed his finger
And went in the goal.
The German crowd cheered and the
English sat down and just sighed.

After disaster struck, England fought back
But couldn't strike the ball back.
At the end, the English cried and
Kevin Keegan resigned.

Matthew Ellis (12)
Mounts Bay School

I RAN THE FOUR HUNDRED METRES

When the gun went off
I jumped off the starting line.
As we were running the crowd was silent.
The nearer I came to the finish line,
The crowd grew louder and louder.
The feeling was great.
I gave a breathtaking performance
In the final 100 metres
And I won a gold medal.

Hayley Hibbert (11)
Mounts Bay School

RUNNING

Here I am,
Standing, waiting
I take my place,
I'm ready now.

Silence . . .
Silence . . .
Bang!

I'm in front,
Yes life is glorious!
Wait, people are
Catching me up
Ahh! I'm behind,
My life is ending!

I feel like heavy weights
Are on my legs.

Wait! I can see the finish line.
I will push myself to the limit.

Hang on! Everybody's slowing
I'm nearly there
Yes, I'm there,
I've won!

It's my moment of glory.
Yessss!

Bethany Stubbings (11)
Mounts Bay School

The Race

The sun beating down on your neck,
The roar of the crowd,
Sudden silence as you wait for the gun,
Your heart pounding,
Your head up, looking towards gold,
Remembering the four years of dedication, practice and pain.

Bang!

The gun goes, your arms and legs moving as fast as possible,
Everything is a blur, apart from the track ahead of you,
You see one person ahead of you,
The last spurt of energy, as the line approaches,
You duck your head, it's all over,
You win gold.

Daniel Freeman (11)
Mounts Bay School

ALONE

I have seen him wander back and forth through
his fields that surround his lonely, isolated farm,
time and time again.
He looks like a lost animal, abandoned by its parents.

His bright blue eyes gaze around, scanning his
surroundings as if looking for predators.
He tramps around his dismal farm, in his old
wrinkled leather boots, that look somewhat
like his bronzed, loose, lifeless skin.

An aggressive wind howls through the decrepit,
crumbling barn,
Sounding like an injured animal, as the barn
door hammers shut, then creaks open on its
rusty hinges, only to slam home once again.

An abandoned air drifts like smoke, lingering
around every corner, lurking in the shadows,
as his lifeline ebbs, getting thinner and
thinner with each passing, hollow day.

Alexandria Allsop (12)
Penair School

THE FISHERMAN

As he and his crew depart from the harbour they pass the rugged cliffs
with speed and agility.
The wind howls like a wounded dog and the sea is a cauldron.
As the boat bounces as if it were on a trampoline so do its passengers.
Their skin is swarthy and their arms muscular.
His massive hands, weather-beaten after years of work hold the
wheel with ease.
The seas calm and look as if they were a smooth piece of silk on
a kitchen table.
The wind becomes an autumn breeze on a warm October evening.
And the sun becomes a warm winter fire in a spacious grange.
The fisherman smiles at the sun as it glistens on the sea.
The fisherman and the sea:
The gentle giants.

Rosie Burrows (12)
Penair School

FISHERMAN'S FIGHT

Today, new supermarkets to supply
They wake up early, the tide is high
The sun looks down on them like a burly boiling balloon
The seaweed streaming long, green hair tangled in the nets
The fish fidget and flounder to get free
The men's hands straining to haul them in
Their face red and beaten by the salty sea some days ago
The nets are in; the catch is removed from the salty waters.

Holly Jarman (12)
Penair School

Passing Days

His face is all wrinkled and crumpled up,
the chestnut hair lightly rests on his shoulder.

Two scraggly, musky dogs follow sluggishly behind,
eating anything they can find on the littered pavement.

Loose fitting clothes hang from his body
like a mouse wearing a top several sizes too big.

Titanic sized glasses sinking down his nose.

The shabby, black and blue bag resting
on a creaking, crooked shoulder.

He's lonely like he doesn't exist.

Kerra Beale (13)
Penair School

THE FARMER

The farmer strains his back, crooked though it already is,
But all of his efforts are in vain,
Falling on ill, unprying eyes,
The hedges are like a wild, untamed mane of a lion.
Despite his illness he still carries on;
His tractor ploughs across the field, like a knife through bread.
Leaden, wavy hair, dangles in his bloodshot eyes,
The arms are flapping, waving to the sky,
As the tiring, old man goes trundling by.

Lee Middleton (12)
Penair School

MYSTERY MAN

His house, a dark, dismal dungeon,
Roaring for repairs.
He mends the house
And gets rid of the one lonely mouse.
His background filled with mysteries.
Nobody ever sees him,
Except when he is shopping or working.
The ground, turned and churned,
No wildlife lives in the trees.
His hands red raw, his house brick-red with paint.
Now his house is gleaming and bright,
The man tired, but his face filled with delight.

Spencer Sanford (12)
Penair School

THE FISHERMAN

The fisherman works all day,
He fights against the huge, powerful waves
And the almighty weather.
His eyes are as red as burning fire,
His hands are hard wearing and as tough as leather.
He labours throughout the day and night.
The evening comes and suddenly the world falls dark around him.
His silhouette stands dark against the misty sky.
Every day it is dark and gloomy;
The waves crash and smash against the huge towering rocks.

Scott Beaumont (12)
Penair School

PATCH

Patch my dog with his long, droopy ears
that drag along the floor like a broom.
His ears are as brown as thick mud
oozing from the river.
His black face with a white stripe down
his wet nose and his green eyes glowing.

Bethany Taylor (12)
Penair School

FARMER

The dark, mysterious lane,
Is a snake-like shape,
Twists and turns so sharp.
Which leads down to the farm,
The farmhouse is decrepit
It is a dusky white colour.

The farmer is old as well,
Has no wife or love,
He is alone, talks to no one,
A tortoise who hides in his shell.

His hair is a grey, dull colour,
So fine and grubby,
And nails full of dirt,
With hands as tough as rubber.

He starts work as soon as the sun,
Works all day never resting,
He is a slave for his animals
But king of the farm.

Kimberley Berryman (12)
Penair School

Ancient Shelly

She plods around the garden,
coming down the ramp.
Her elephant feet with scales like a snake,
appear from her camouflaged shell.
Next pokes a head, like a fish coming up for air,
as she makes her way to the shaded trees,
it's a jungle as she slides like a snail,
through the slippery grass.
She is a stone on wheels,
as the birds sing above her on the tops of the high trees.
Her golden dish filled with a fresh juicy salad
soon goes, as she crunches into the green crisp lettuce.
Digging with her tiger claws,
trying to get under the wooden frame,
like a prisoner trying to escape.
She is a shell on the beach with shapes and darkened colours,
the sound of the herding cattle, drift through the windy branches.
As ancient delicate Shelly goes up the carpet ramp,
curls up in newspaper and tucks herself goodnight.

Carly Geach (12)
Penair School

VILLAGE BOY

Ashley is a poor village boy,
Who lives in a small run-down cottage,
The cottage walls are crumpled like a stepped-on biscuit.
The roof is half-thatched
and is falling apart like an edge of a cliff.
The windows are broken and cracked
like a boat that has just come back from a storm.
It is a spider's paradise with cobwebs everywhere.
Ashley does not care because he has lived like this all of his life.
Ashley is run down like his cottage.
He has one pair of patched-up trousers
and a jumper the colour of burnt ashes.
This is all he has.

Kerry Skeggs ((12)
Penair School

OLD MAN

His distinctive eyes,
sparkle like the sun,
his skin as dark as a brown log.
He walks his drooling bulldog,
which pulls him away from his dreams.
The tugging of the lead brings him back to reality,
his sighing hips,
moving slowly side to side.
The howling wind joins the sun,
the green grass floating,
up towards the sky.
The birds swoop around the trees.
The wind is calling out his name.
The air is floating around like a huge balloon,
covering the world.

Kensa Allen (12)
Penair School

LEWIS BRIDGER

The jungle stands still while hunters will kill
Those poor birds flying so high in the sky.
The monkeys swing and the scary lions bring
Their baby cubs a bulky dinner for spring.
The spiders weave webs as bats hang in the flooded jungle.
In America it stands.

Lewis Bridger (13)
Penair School

The Fisherman

Sunshine or rain, the fisherman is out,
Trying to get his catch of squid and trout.
The wind is howling through the sails
And the seas are roaring as waves curve and crash.
When you're fishing you feel grand
Pulling in your heavy catch.
When you're fishing way out at sea
Everything is calm and there's lots of fish.

Chris Tolley (12)
Penair School

The Fisherman

He sails in his boat, like a bird on top of the water.
The ocean is his world
And the fish are his life
The water is his existence
On it every day he makes it his friend.
The sea gives him energy,
To continue on throughout his life at sea of
toughness and adversity.

Alex Winkworth (13)
Penair School

THE FISHERMAN

The waves overlap each other,
like a horse leaping over a jump.
Sunshine or rain, windy or cloudy
the fisherman is halfway out to sea
on his bobbing boat,
trying to get his catch.
The wind is howling as the air
is whistling through the sails.

Natasha Waller (12)
Penair School

The Farmer

Standing on the granite platform, staring out to the setting sun,
His torn, lined, olive jacket flaps in the wind
And the trees in the distance gesture back.
His tanned, leathery face looks like a content elephant
As he squints to get a wider view of the country below him.
The assorted group of cows he can see are like a box of chocolates
And the crumbling church in the distance
Resembles a broken egg, nestled in a modern city.

Spencer Woods (12)
Penair School

The Gardener

Wind, sun or rain, the gardener is out,
Brambles lashing at his sturdy arms like the lions chewing their prey.
His arched back, pressing forward towards the ground.
As he lifts his spade, his back creaks as though it's going to snap.
Blues, reds, lavenders and scarlets surround him in beds of colour
as the sea surrounds a ship.

There's a little patch of daisies shooting up through the crust
of the ground.
His tender fingers care for them.
Any weeds are cleared away by dustpan hands so flower seeds can
shoot unharmed.
New leaves upon the trees, the old have fallen away and have been
scooped up to decay.

Alice Martin (13)
Penair School

REMMINGTON

He's swift on his feet,
his body as hard as steel,
just standing there, on the grass-covered
fields and lovely open flowers.
His long grey tail, like a moon in the
skylit summer's evening.
His broad swaying mane like a tree
in the wind.
His fine legs swooping as he moves
like leaves falling from a tree in autumn.
His hard, clumpy feet, hitting the ragged,
hard ground at every floating pace.
He walks and wanders upon the gravelled footpaths,
like a lost child in a dream.
His beautiful whinnying neigh, like
bluebells bashing against each other, in the summer's breeze.

Rebecca Gofton (12)
Penair School

DEEP IN THE RAINFOREST

Deep in the rainforest,
The equatorial temperature makes the air sticky and humid.
The lush, green vegetation is wet underfoot,
Gigantic trees tower above.
The vibrant sound of humming birds fills the damp atmosphere,
Sucking juicy nectar from radiant red flowers.
The distant howl of monkeys echoes through the dense forest,
Swinging energetically through the tall trees.
A rustle on the ground as an iguana scuttles past,
Camouflaged by the different shades of green.
Further into the forest an army of ants march across the
uneven ground,
Working together to find food to survive.
All of a sudden, a loud piercing noise interrupts the tranquillity,
Crashing trees destroy the animals' habitats, soon there will be
nothing left.

Catherine Rollins (14)
The Roseland Community School

STARVING AFRICA

Extreme hunger rules the diseased plains
Robbing the lives of the young and old
Sorrow and suffering quickens its
pace across the poverty-stricken
land.
Walking miles upon miles
in the burning heat, each
day for fresh water,
just to find a dried-up well.
No medicine, nor food:
education has to come last.
The war ended
years ago, but
refugees still
straggle to survive.
Bones, covered
with only a weak
wafer-thin layer
of skin, stand
out from the
starving
skeletons.
Our
selfishness,
greed
causes the
misery and
poverty
of these
people.
Their hope
won't
last long!

Rhiannon Pring (15)
The Roseland Community School

READY TO CHEER

1.30pm it's time to leave,
everyone excited, ready to cheer.
In the car we all bundle in, all set
to go with our hats and scarves.
Up the motorway, the car goes,
with toots and horns as we go.
With moans and groans of kids in the back,
'Hey Dad, are we nearly there yet?'
We pull up to park, but will we find a space?
'Quick, there's one or we're gonna be late!'
Buy a programme from outside,
hand over ticket and get inside.
Hear the crowd cheering as we walk in and
quickly find our seats to sit and watch and win.
As the players enter the pitch,
all the fans stand and cheer.
It's still nil-nil, and it's gone half-time.
Will we ever win, I think in my mind.
With a quick run from Ready and a shot from Sinclair
the ball goes in and everyone cries with cheer.
With a smile on their faces, the players walk in,
ready to shower and wash their hair.
It's gone 5.30 and the fans are happy
going home to see their family.
As the stadium doors shut for another week,
all is quiet, for now at least.

Natalie Magowan (14)
The Roseland Community School

SPACE

Space seems impossible through a window,
Looking up it doesn't seem real,
The sky once blue is lined with the gentle twinkle of glistening objects,
Each one individual, unique and on its own,
Each one special, each one admired for its beauty as it makes up space as we know it,
The changing shape of the white eye fascinates and confuses.
How can we understand the universe if our world still puzzles?

Amy Sampson (15)
The Roseland Community School

My World

The galaxy is huge;
Millions of tiny, flickering fairy lights,
Balls of gas, rocks and ice,
Circuiting, surrounding.

We are one of those tiny rocks,
Spinning, round and round,
We have life forms,
Some better than others.

We are one in a million,
So why abuse it,
Polluting, wasting, ignoring the obvious?

The ozone is thinning,
We are not listening,
Our rock is heating,
Ready to *pop!*

This probably won't happen,
Until we find another excuse,
But it won't work,
It will finally happen,
Someday, somehow.

Laura Brockhurst (14)
The Roseland Community School

Bonfire Night

In the distance, shafts of colour cascade over the horizon.
Sparks dance and skip in the air
then fade in the forever blue darkness of the
night sky.
The wind pulls the faint voices up into the flames,
licking furiously at the solar system above, stretching to grasp
a myriad stars that decorate the blue surroundings.
A whistle parts the sea of stars.
It overpowers the stars, the fire, and the deep night sky,
erupting into sequins, shimmering diamonds, which drop
shyly towards Earth as if waiting for the right moment to interrupt.
But again the sea of stars close in.
The sparks return to their merry dance.
The fire flickers in the sparkling eyes of enchanted children,
and the dark blue forever sky draws in around landscape
beyond.

Amy Leech (14)
The Roseland Community School

MOVING ON

Millions of people
On our planet Earth,
Living separate lives
With no value, no worth.

War, murder,
Violence, crime.
We should join together,
All live as one.

People start talking,
Memories are shared.
The good deeds are done,
Peace is declared.

Moving forward,
The time ticks on
As we enter the year
2001.

Marie Dalgarno (14)
The Roseland Community School

My Hideaway Place

Stormy seas crash wildly, against the Cornish coast.
Moist spray rebounds quickly, as if it were a painful shock.
Pitter-patter of the rain, it hits the bouncing boat.
The coldness almost scary, creates shivers on my spine.

Patches of multi-greens, for miles can be seen.
Rough jagged coastlines, stretch high into the sky.
Whipping sand soars through the air at speed
And the whistling wind, that almost wraps around your ears.

This is where I like to hide
To get away from all the worries
To be alone and undisturbed
That is where I like to go.

Rebekah Gibbons (14)
The Roseland Community School